Slim Goodbody's
GOOD HEALTH GUIDES

AVOIDING INJURIES

By Slim Goodbody

Photos by Chris Pinchbeck
Illustrations by Ben McGinnis

Consultant: Marlene Melzer-Lange, M.D.
Pediatric Emergency Medicine
Medical College of Wisconsin
Milwaukee, Wisconsin

GARETH**STEVENS**
GS PUBLISHING
A Member of the WRC Media Family of Companies

Please visit our web site at: www.garethstevens.com
For a free color catalog describing Gareth Stevens Publishing's
list of high-quality books and multimedia programs, call
1-800-542-2595 (USA) or 1-800-387-3178 (Canada).
Gareth Stevens Publishing's fax: (414) 332-3567.

Library of Congress Cataloging-in-Publication Data

Burstein, John.
  Avoiding injuries / by Slim Goodbody.
    p. cm. — (Slim Goodbody's good health guides)
  Includes bibliographical references and index.
  ISBN-13: 978-0-8368-7739-7 (lib. bdg.)
    1. Accidents—Prevention—Juvenile literature. 2. Children's accidents—
Prevention—Juvenile literature. 3. Health—Juvenile literature.
  4. Safety education—Juvenile literature. I. Title.
  RA777.B8744   2007
  613.60835-dc22   2006032764

This edition first published in 2007 by
Gareth Stevens Publishing
A Member of the WRC Media Family of Companies
330 West Olive Street, Suite 100
Milwaukee, WI 53212 USA

Photos: Chris Pinchbeck, Pinchbeck Photography
Page 24 (left): Courtesy of USDA
Illustrations: Ben McGinnis, Adventure Advertising

Managing editor: Valerie J. Weber
Art direction and design: Tammy West

Printed in Canada

1 2 3 4 5 6 7 8 9 10 10 09 08 07 06

TABLE OF CONTENTS

Words that appear in the glossary are printed in **boldface** type the first time they occur in the text.

The Black-and-Blue Blues

Sometimes something happens,
And your body takes a bruising
A broken arm, a cut, or burn
Or major black-and-bluesing.
You never know the time or place,
You never know just how,
But you can bet an accident
Will leave you yelling "OW!"

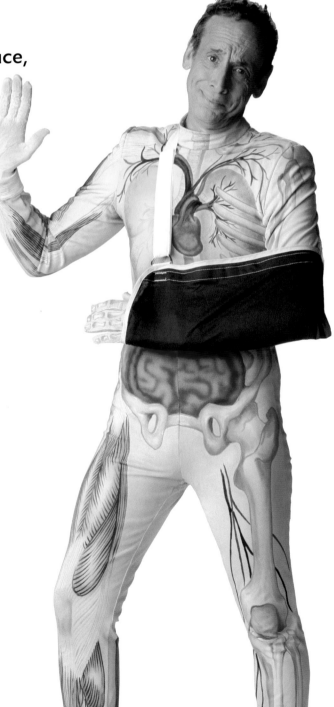

No matter how careful you are, accidents happen. You might trip on a stair, slip on some ice, or flip off a skateboard. You could be sitting outside reading and get stung by a bee. You could be eating indoors and choke on some food. You could be playing with your cat and get a bad scratch. You might even be asleep and roll out of bed.

There are many ways to get hurt and many parts of your body that can be injured. You can cut your skin, **strain** a muscle, or break a bone.

Luckily, these things do not happen very often. When they do, your body has an amazing ability to heal itself. Let's find out what happens when you get hurt and how your wonderful body fixes itself.

Watch where you are going!

Something to Think About

Many accidents happen when you are not paying attention. You are doing one thing but thinking about something else. You can prevent these accidents by focusing on what is right in front of you. Another reason accidents happen is because people take risks. If you do something dangerous, you are more likely to get hurt, so play it safe.

Bones, Moans, and Groans

Your bones are tough and strong. They can take lots of stress and strain. If you fall hard enough or are in a bad accident, though, your bones can break.

A broken bone is called a **fracture**. Not every fracture breaks a bone completely in two, however. Sometimes only one side of the bone breaks. Breaks like these are more common for children. Kids have softer bones than adults, and their bones bend a bit more easily. One-sided breaks tend to happen in the middle of long bones, like those in your arms or legs.

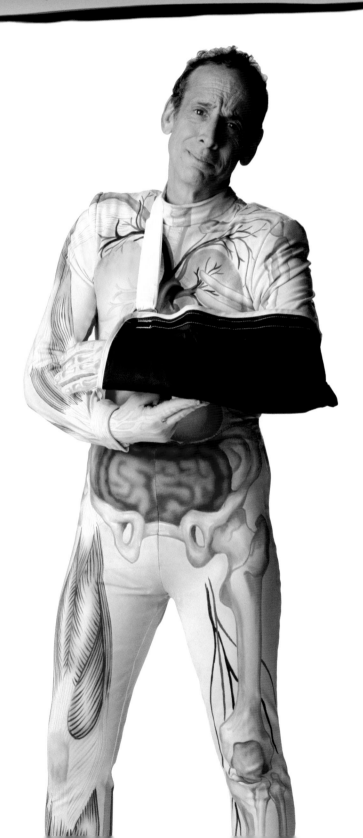

In the following list, fractures 1 and 2 are more common for children.
Fractures 3 and 4 are more common for grown-ups.

 **1** Greenstick fractures occur when one side of the bone breaks, but the other side only bends. This break tends to happen in the middle of long bones, like those in the arms or legs.

 **2** Torus fractures happen when one side of the bone bends in on itself and raises a little bump or buckle. The other side of the bone does not break.

 **3** Simple fractures occur when the bone breaks all the way through but does not poke through the skin

 **4** Compound fractures happen when the bone breaks all the way through and pokes through the skin.

Something to Think About

The most common place for you to get a fracture is in your arm — your wrist, forearm, or above your elbow. When you take a tumble, it is natural to throw your hands in front of you to stop your fall. If you land wrong or land too hard, a bone can break.

Good News: Good as New

One of the most amazing things about a broken bone is that it can heal itself. It can grow back together as good as new!

If you think you have a broken bone, a doctor will take an X-ray. This picture looks different than the ones you take with a regular camera. It shows a doctor your bones. The doctor can see what is wrong and what needs to be done.

The X-ray will show if the bone is broken all the way through. It will also let the doctor see if the two broken ends are lined up with each other. If they are, the bone can grow together evenly. If they are not, a doctor can line them up during an operation.

When the bones are in the right place, your doctor will wrap a cast around them. A cast is a special kind of bandage that keeps your bones from moving while

they heal. A cast has two layers — a soft cotton inner layer that rests against your skin and a hard outer layer to protect your bones from being hurt again.

Then, your body gets to work on healing. Here is what happens:

1 When the bone breaks, it cuts nearby **blood vessels**.

2 The blood leaks into the break and dries. This is called a **blood clot**. The clot acts like weak glue. It helps hold the bones together.

3 The blood brings material to repair the bone ends at the break and to help them grow toward each other.

4 The ends finally reach each other, and the bone heals as good as new.

It can take as little as three weeks or as long as a couple of months for the bones to heal. Once the bones have healed, the doctor cuts the cast off carefully with a saw.

Something to Think About

You can help prevent bone breaks. Here is how:

1 Buckle your seatbelt. Automobile accidents (and falls) cause more broken bones than anything else.

2 Drink milk. It contains Vitamin D and calcium, both of which are good for building strong bones.

3 Get lots of exercise. Jumping rope, jogging, and running are really good for making your bones stronger.

Strains and Sprains

If you like to run around or play sports, you will probably get a strain or a **sprain** at some time. A strain is an injury to a muscle. It can happen when you push too hard and stretch a muscle too far. You might get a muscle strain if you lift something that is very heavy.

Sprains are injuries to **ligaments**. A ligament is a special kind of **tissue** that holds bones together at **joints**. A joint is the place where two bones meet. You will end up with a sprain if your ligaments get stretched too far or they tear.

Sprains are much worse than strains. They hurt more and take longer to heal.

Your doctor may even have you wear a **splint** or a cast for a while so you will not move it.

Both strains and sprains cause swelling. The injured area looks bruised and feel tender. Doctors have come up with a four-step way to help you feel better.

It is called **RICE** – **R-I-C-E**. Here is how it works:

1 **R stands for Rest**. Do not use the part of your body that is hurt.

2 **I stands for Ice**. Put ice or cold packs on the injury every few hours for the first 2 days. Do not use heat because it causes more pain and swelling.

3 **C stands for Compression**. Wrap the injury snugly — but not too tightly — with an elastic bandage for at least 2 days to reduce swelling.

4 **E stands for Elevate**. Keep the injured part up. Raising it will also help reduce swelling.

Cold muscles get hurt more easily than warm ones. You can help prevent strains and sprains by doing some gentle stretches before you exercise. Movement gets your blood flowing faster and warms up your muscles.

Something to Think About

Some children get pains in their legs at night. These aches are sometimes called growing pains. Doctors think they are muscle pains caused by being active during the day. You can help: Put a heating pad on the muscles that hurt, do some gentle leg stretching, or have someone rub the sore spots. Growing pains usually go away by morning.

Skin + Injury = Skinjury

Your skin is a lot softer than your bones. Skin gets injured more often than any other part of your body. It can get cut, scraped, scratched, bruised, or burned.

Luckily, skin has a terrific ability to repair itself. When it gets hurt, it begins healing right away.

Here is what happens when you get a cut or deep scratch:

1 Tiny blood vessels in your skin get torn, and you start to bleed.

2 The blood helps clean the wound by washing **germs** away.

3 The blood dries and gets sticky, forming a clot.

4 The clot stops the bleeding.

5 The clot gets harder. It forms a crust over the wound, called a scab.

6 Under the scab, new skin grows.

7 **White blood cells** attack and destroy any germs that sneak into the wound.

8 In a week or two, your new skin is ready, and the scab falls off.

You can help your skin heal. Here is how:

1 Clean the cut with soap and water even if washing the cut stings a little.

2 Press down on the wound with a clean cloth or **gauze** pad for a few minutes. This pressure will help stop the bleeding.

3 Put some germ-fighting medicine on the wound.

4 Put a bandage on the wound to keep it clean.

5 If a scab forms, do not pick at it. Let it fall off by itself.

Always ask your mom, dad, or another grown-up for help. If the cut is very deep or wide, a doctor must use stitches to hold the edges together.

Something to Think About

Many skin injuries are caused by sharp objects that make a hole in your skin. These injuries are called **puncture** wounds. They may not bleed a lot, but they can be very serious. You need to clean them well, and be sure to tell your parents right away. One way to help prevent a lot of puncture wounds is to wear shoes when you are outside. Shoes have rubber or leather soles that keep sharp objects from sticking into the bottoms of your feet.

Bumps and Lumps

Chances are that if you look carefully at your body, you will find a bruise or two somewhere on your skin. Most children get lots of bumps and lumps as they grow up. It is a natural part of childhood.

Bruises go through colorful changes as they heal.

Here is what happens:

1 There are lots of small blood vessels running through and under your skin.

2 A good hard bump or bang will break some of these blood vessels.

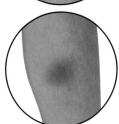

3 Blood leaks out and collects under your skin.

4 As the blood builds up, the bruise may swell bigger.

5 At first, the bruise will look red or purplish.

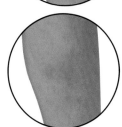

6 In 2 or 3 days, it will start looking blue or blackish.

7 After a week or so, it may turn yellow or greenish.

8 After another week, it will turn a light brown.

9 It will get lighter and lighter as it fades away.

The color changes mean that your body is breaking down blood trapped in your skin.

If you get a bruise, here are some things you can do:

1 Stop using the part of your body that was hurt.

2 Put a cold pack on the bruise for 20 minutes. A cold pack can be made by wrapping a washcloth around a plastic bag that is filled with ice. A cold pack can also be just a bag of frozen peas or frozen corn. The cold will help stop the swelling.

Something to Think About

Help your body out. When you are riding your bike, skating, skateboarding, or playing sports, wear safety equipment. That way, you can avoid many bruises altogether!

Top to Toe – Oh No!

Your body can get hurt in many different places. Sometimes your head or feet can get banged up. Here are three of the most common injuries to these places:

Black Eye

A black eye is not an injury to your eye itself. It is a colorful bruise that forms around your eye. Here is what happens:

1 The skin around your eye is loose.

2 If you get hit in the face or head, blood collects there.

3 The injury causes the area to swell up and change color.

If you put a cold pack on the area right away, the cold will help keep down the swelling.

Most black eyes are not very serious. They will heal on their own in a few days as the swelling goes down and the color fades away.

Bloody Nose

Nosebleeds can be messy and painful, but they are usually not very serious. If you get a nosebleed, here are some tips:

1 Sit up or stand. Do not lie down.

2 Tip your head forward, so the blood will not run down your throat.

3 Pinch the soft part of your nose together between your thumb and index finger.

4 Breathe in and out through your mouth for 10 minutes without stopping.

5 Use a tissue or a damp washcloth to catch any blood.

6 Once the bleeding has stopped, do not bend over for a few hours or rub, pick, or blow your nose.

Stubbed Toe

Have you ever stubbed your toe or slammed your finger in a door? It can be very painful, and sometimes you can lose your

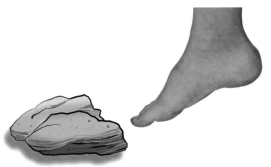

nail. Luckily, it will grow back again. To help with the pain, soak the injury in cold water as soon as possible. The coldness will reduce the pain and swelling. If the injury looks really bad, your parents will need to call the doctor.

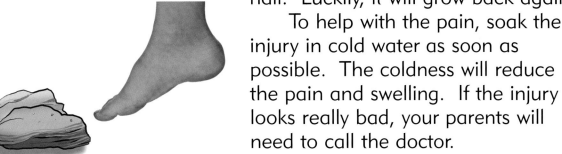

Something to Think About

Nails are made from the same material as your hair and the top layer of your skin. Nails do not grow as quickly as your hair. If you lose your whole fingernail, it will take about four months to regrow. A lost toenail will take longer to regrow — about six months.

A Bang to the Brain

If your head gets hit really hard, your brain can get knocked against the inside wall of your bony skull. This blow can cause an injury called a head injury. A head injury can be mild or very serious. It changes the way your brain works for a while.

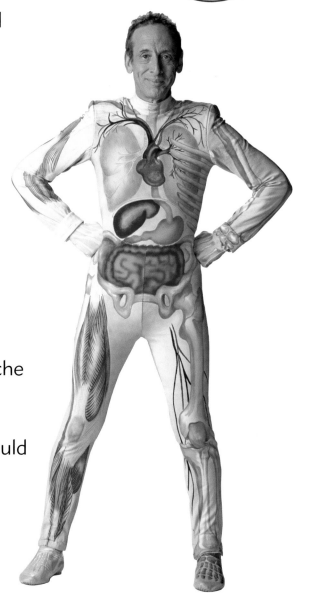

Here is what can happen if you get a mild head injury:

1 You will probably feel dizzy, dazed, and confused for a while.

2 You may feel sick to your stomach and throw up.

3 Your vision may be blurry.

4 You may even lose some of your memory and forget what happened right before and right after you got hurt.

5 You may have a mild headache for a few days or longer.

If the head injury is bad, you could become unaware of everything around you. You will probably need to go to the hospital.

No matter what, if you get a head injury, you need to see a doctor to make sure everything is healing properly. While you are recovering, take it easy at school and at home. You will need to wait until your doctor says it is okay to start playing sports again.

Be patient — this may take a few weeks or months.

Something to Think About

The most common causes for head injuries are car accidents, bike crashes, playground falls, or sports injuries. The best way to prevent a head injury is by taking care of your head. Here is how:

1 Always wear a helmet when riding your bike, skateboarding, skating, skiing, and snowboarding.

2 Always wear a seatbelt in a car. If you are ten years old or younger or weigh less than 80 pounds (36 kilograms), you probably need a booster seat. If you sit on the seat itself, the seatbelt will not fit correctly.

3 Obey safety rules when crossing the street. Always use a crosswalk. Always look left, then right, then left again.

4 Wear the right safety equipment when playing sports.

Hot!!

Have you ever stepped into a bath that is too hot? Then you know that fire is not the only thing that can burn your skin. Electricity, chemicals, and the Sun can also cause burns.

Your skin has different layers called the outer, middle, and inner. The deeper the layer of skin that a burn reaches, the worse the burn is.

First-degree burns are the least serious. Only the outer layer of skin is harmed. Your skin gets red and tender. The burned area may swell. It is painful.

Second-degree burns go deeper. The first and second layers of skin get burned. The skin gets much, much redder, and **blisters** form. It is very, very painful.

Third-degree burns are the most serious of all. The skin is burned all the way through. Some of the skin may be completely destroyed. The burn can even go through muscles and bone. Third-degree burns are so serious that people must go to the hospital to get help. Amazing as it sounds, third-degree burns do not hurt. When the skin is destroyed so badly, no feeling remains.

You can take care of most first- and second-degree burns at home. Here are some basic first-aid tips:

1 Run cool (not cold) water over the burned area or hold a clean, cold cloth on the burn until the pain fades a bit. The coldness will also reduce swelling.

2 Do not use ice. Ice can hurt the burned skin and cause the burn to take longer to heal.

3 Be sure the burned area is clean.

4 Protect the burned area with a loose bandage.

5 Ask your doctor if burn ointment will help.

6 Do not use grease or butter to cover the burn.

7 If blisters form, do not break them.

8 After the burn heals, keep the area covered with **sunscreen** when you are out in the sun.

Something to Think About

Not all burns are caused by heat. Frostbite is a burn that is caused by cold! If you are out for too long in freezing weather, here is what can happen:

1 The skin of your nose, ears, fingers, or toes gets very, very cold.

2 Your blood cannot flow freely to the cold areas.

3 Your skin gets red and starts to swell.

4 Blisters form.

If you do not get warm soon, the frozen skin can die.

Lots of Spots

If you suddenly get covered with lots of spots, you might have a skin **rash**. A skin rash can look scaly, bumpy, red, or swollen. It can make your skin feel dry and itchy. You can get a skin rash by touching plants such as poison ivy, poison oak, and poison sumac.

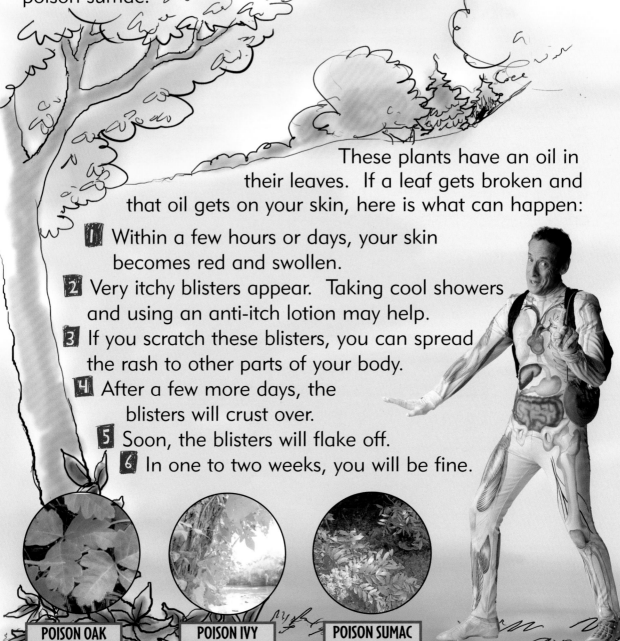

These plants have an oil in their leaves. If a leaf gets broken and that oil gets on your skin, here is what can happen:

1 Within a few hours or days, your skin becomes red and swollen.

2 Very itchy blisters appear. Taking cool showers and using an anti-itch lotion may help.

3 If you scratch these blisters, you can spread the rash to other parts of your body.

4 After a few more days, the blisters will crust over.

5 Soon, the blisters will flake off.

6 In one to two weeks, you will be fine.

POISON OAK

POISON IVY

POISON SUMAC

Poison oak, poison ivy, and poison sumac can be found in many places. They can grow in the woods, in the park, or even in your own backyard!

Here are some things you can do to protect yourself:

1 Learn what these poisonous plants look like so you can stay away from them.

2 If you are in places where these plants might grow, cover up in long pants and long sleeves.

3 If you get the oil on your skin, try to shower it off right away. Use plenty of soap.

4 Do not take a bath because the oil can get in the bathwater and spread to other parts of your body.

Something to Think About

Rashes can be caused by many different things. Some people get rashes because they eat certain foods, such as peanuts, or take certain medicines, such as penicillin. Some people get rashes from wearing clothing made from certain materials such as wool. Most people have had a least one rash in their life — when they were babies and got diaper rash!

Stings on Wings

We share our world with billions of insects. Many of them bite or sting. Most are little, but if they sting or bite you, it sure can hurt.

There are thousands of different kinds of mosquitoes. They come in many different sizes and colors. Female mosquitoes use your blood to help them lay eggs and make more mosquitoes. First, they bite you, then they suck your blood. A chemical in their spit makes the bite really itch.

When you get bitten, a round bump forms around the bite. This bump is called a wheal, or welt. It is pinkish red on the edges and white in the middle. The wheal itches a lot. Soon, the wheal fades away, but the itching does not.

The best thing you can do to keep mosquitoes away is to use an insect **repellent**. Your parents or other adults can spray or rub this liquid or lotion on your skin or clothes. Mosquitoes hate it.

Some insects do not bite. They sting!

Bees, wasps, and hornets will sting you if they get upset. The sting feels like a shot you get at the doctor's office. Often, the insect will leave its stinger behind, stuck in your skin! The area around it will probably feel hot and itchy. Soon you will get a red bump.

If you get bitten or stung, here is what you can do:

1 Tell a grown-up.

2 If there is a stinger left in your skin, have an adult scrape it off.

3 Wash the area with soap and water.

4 Put an ice pack on it to keep down the swelling.

5 Putting on anti-itch cream or lotion may help with bites.

Something to Think About

Other insects that cause trouble are lice. Lice are not nice! They live in your hair and make your scalp feel really itchy. Once you get lice, it is hard to get rid of them. It takes special shampoos, combs, and lots of time. Lice travel from person to person. You can help protect yourself from lice by not sharing combs, brushes, hats, scarves, barrettes, hair ties, towels, and helmets with others.

To Choke Is No Joke!

Sometimes food goes where it does not belong. That can make you choke. You may have heard somebody say, "The food went down the wrong pipe." Here is what that means:

1 At the back of your throat are two tubes right next to each other.

2 One tube leads to your lungs, and the other leads to your stomach.

3 The tube leading to your lungs is called your windpipe.

4 When you swallow, the top of the windpipe gets covered by a flap of skin. This flap keeps food, drinks, or other objects from getting in.

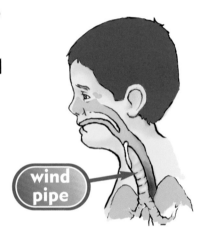

wind pipe

5 Once in a while, things slip past the flap and go down "the wrong pipe" — the windpipe.

Most of the time, this is no big deal. You just cough, forcing the food or drink back up. Sometimes, however, the windpipe gets completely blocked, and you cannot cough anything out. You cannot even breathe! If you cannot breathe, you cannot live. That is what makes choking so serious.

Here are some ways to prevent choking when eating:

1 Cut all your food into small pieces. Small pieces are harder to choke on.

2 Sit down while you eat. If you eat standing up, you may not be paying enough attention to what you are chewing.

3 Do not play games with your food, such as catching popcorn in your mouth. When you catch food in your mouth, it can get stuck in your throat.

4 Do not talk with your mouth full. Chew and swallow before you talk or laugh. If you laugh while you are eating, you might accidentally suck food to the back of your throat where it can get stuck.

5 Be careful when eating foods like hot dogs, nuts, grapes, raw carrots, popcorn, and hard or gooey candy. These foods are easy to choke on.

If you see somebody choking, yell for help right away or call 911 on the phone. There is no time to lose!

There is also a special way to help someone who is choking. This action was invented by a doctor. It is called the Heimlich **maneuver**. It cannot be taught in a book like this, but your parents or teachers can learn it and then teach it to you.

Something to Think About

Choking is not just caused by food getting caught in your windpipe. Many children choke on coins, pen caps, balloons, beads, erasers, batteries, and other small objects that they swallow. Never put anything in your mouth that does not belong there.

Always remember,
Your body is strong
And it can repair
Most things that go wrong.

Accidents happen,
Each life has a few.
But try to prevent them
From happening to you.

Have you heard these sayings?

"Watch your step."
"Think before you act."
"Look before you leap."

They all have one thing in common — good simple advice. That advice is "Be careful and be safe." If you take this advice, you can avoid a lot of problems.

Nobody can get through life without accidents, but you can reduce their number and danger if you:

1 Avoid risky behavior such as not buckling your seatbelt, not wearing a bike helmet, or not staying a safe distance away from a fire.

2 Learn the ways that accidents can happen.

3 Pay close attention to whatever you are doing.

4 Use the right safety equipment for whatever you are doing.

5 Learn what to do to help yourself and others if an accident happens.

Remember, you can stay safe and avoid the Black-and-Blue Blues!

Glossary

blisters — raised areas of the skin that contain liquid

blood clot — blood cells that cling together and thicken

blood vessels — small hoselike tubes through which blood travels all over the body

compression — the state of having something pressed or squeezed together. Injured parts of the body are wrapped with an elastic bandage to produce compression, which helps keep swelling down.

elevate — to raise up

fracture — a broken bone

gauze — a cotton cloth that comes in pads or rolls

germs — tiny living things that can often cause disease

joints — places in the body where two bones come together

ligaments — tough, elastic bands of muscle-like tissue that bind bones together at joints

maneuver — a well planned-out series of actions

puncture — a hole in the skin made by a sharp point

rash — itchy, bumpy, red spots that break out on skin

repellent — a chemical spray or lotion that is used to keep insects away from skin

splint — a device made to protect a body part and to keep it from moving

sprain — an injury caused by too much stretching or tearing of ligaments

strain — to hurt a muscle by overusing it or putting too much pressure on it

sunscreen — a skin lotion or cream that prevents sunburn

tissue — cells of the same shape and kind that group together

white blood cells — special cells in blood that fight germs

For More Information

BOOKS

Broken Bones. My Health (series). Alvin Silverstein, Virginia B. Silverstein, and Laura Silverstein Nunn (Franklin Watts)

Head and Brain Injuries. Diseases and People (series). Elaine Landau (Enslow Publishing)

The Kids' Guide to First Aid: All About Bruises, Burns, Stings, Sprains and Other Ouches. A Williamson Kids™ Can Book (series). Karen Buhler Gale (Williamson Publishing Company)

Kids to the Rescue: First Aid Techniques for Kids. Maribeth Boelts and Darwin Boelts (Parenting Press)

WEB SITES

Kids Health for Kids
www.kidshealth.org/kid/ill_injure
Check out this Web site for information on all kinds of injuries and illnesses.

Leaf It Alone: Plants to Stay Away From
www.lanakids.com/plants.html
Learn about the kinds of plants that can give you an itchy rash, how to avoid them, and what to do if you get a rash.

Slim Goodbody
www.slimgoodbody.com
Discover loads of fun and free downloads for kids and parents.

Note to educators and parents: The publisher has carefully reviewed these Web sites to ensure that they are suitable for children. Many Web sites change frequently, however, and Gareth Stevens, Inc., cannot guarantee that a site's future contents will continue to meet our high standards of quality and educational value. Be advised that children should be closely supervised whenever they access the Internet.

Index

About the Author

John Burstein (also known as Slim Goodbody) has been entertaining and educating children for over thirty years. His programs have been broadcast on CBS, PBS, Nickelodeon, USA, and Discovery. Over the years, he has developed programs with the American Association for Health Education, the American Academy of Pediatrics, the National YMCA, the President's Council on Physical Fitness and Sports, the International Reading Association, and the National Council of Teachers of Mathematics. He has won numerous awards including the Parent's Choice Award and the President's Council's Fitness Leader Award. Currently, Mr. Burstein tours the country with his multimedia live show "Bodyology." For more information, please visit slimgoodbody.com.